Destructive and Unnecessary

Owen Fitzpatrick

Presentation by *BookLeaf Publishing*

Web: www.bookleafpub.com

E-mail: info@bookleafpub.com

ISBN: 9789357440745

First edition 2023

ACKNOWLEDGEMENT

I would like to thank my good buddy, Liam for his services as a poet consultant.

PREFACE

The poems you are about to read all come from something within my life. Whether it's something I suffer from or am fascinated by, everything can be attached to me in some way, shape, or form. Many poems and ideas came from personal challenges that I decided to set on myself as limitation breeds innovation, but I can see in some cases where the themes and backgrounds of certain poems can be seen as dark. I do wish to state that while poems have the wonderful openness that leads to a variety of debates and discussions on their meaning, it can also be easy to misinterpret a word or phrase that could be seen in a way I never intended. Know that I never mean harm.

As a writer who isn't a poet first, this challenge provided me an opportunity to explore something new and change the way I think. Writing 21 poems in 21 days, the hardest part was finding 21 topics. Growing up introverted, I wasn't exposed to too much. You might notice some of the poems blending together, but I see it as a way to show that they can connect, and prove that they came from the same place. This challenge helped me look more within myself and view my character through a new lens. I hope to retain what I learned going forward as ways to improve my writing.

Divide and conquer

i have Awoken in The Night
as Pressure tries to Break Me Down
Relentless in this Reality
i finally Confess about You.

my Pride will Rip You Apart
there's No Way Out and No Way Home
The Other Side is Where I Belong
Taking Over is easy when you are Hollow

Break My Body and i will Bleed
suffering Scars by the Million
The Crown is covered in Filthy Stains
and All It Takes is a Death In The Family

Psycho is a State Of Mind
Monster is Beyond Human
Never Alone with my Demons
only Broken Statues are By My Side

it is Never Enough to Stand Tall
Move Mountains or take Flight
The Poison is how to Understand Pain
just one DOMINO away from WAR

my Heart Of Stone will Mourn No More
See Me Now and Say My Name
it's Into The Dark in my Darkest Hour
Set It On Fire and Burn

i have Returned completely Victorious
no longer Next In Line for The Grand Line
i have become God in this Domain
Believe It and Bow Down

OUTCAST with all this POWER
So Afraid i was Born For This
i chose All For One instead of One For All
yet i am Holding On for The One Who Knocks

Turn The Page finally To The End
all in a Flash but i Just Begun
please Find Your Way just Beyond The Walls
my Lips Closed until you Hear Me

i always hated goodbyes

Distractions

My mind is filled with creation.
My hands desire the action.
My heart is filled with determination,
But I'm surrounded by all these distractions.

My sword clinging to clash.
My pen trembling for traction.
My hammer must wait to bash,
as my spoon consumes a distraction.

I yearn to be an explorer,
but inside is the main attraction.
I learn instead a new adventure,
A full library of distractions.

I fail to fill the holes
that require satisfaction.
I pass to halt my goals
with everyday distractions.

For all that needs to be done,
It is all merely a fraction.
For my wants are never none,
Maybe I need the distraction.

Claw Machine

The many eyes inside you greet me when I enter.
Watch as I consume grease to settle with last night's alcohol.
Breakfast is over.
My stomach full, my wallet nearly empty.
My last twenty for the bill and there you are waiting for me.
My paycheck spent on food, yet you still remain the one dollar.
No singles, but four quarters shine between the leather.
The coins slot in and the game begins.
My eyes catch a colorful palette of fur slightly buried among a sea of gray.
I have limited time, so I make my choice.
My mind could've calculated the trajectory with all possible predictions.
My hand could've maneuvered millimeter by millimeter for the perfect angle.
The claw could've descended onto what I believed to be a perfect moment.
But I knew fate would say no.
My aim probably would've been ever so off,
leaving the metal fingers to only caress the soft,
beautiful face of the grand prize.

I instead leave with the easygoing gray bear with
cheap fabric barely holding it together.
Once again, I leave without the grand prize.
Only satisfied I left with any prize.

Dear Death

Dumb doesn't do diligence and describe the degenerate who dares defy my disorderly developments. Doesn't take a detective to derive the deliberate deeds done to me. Dotting the i's, details don't add up. Blind sees my due date delays from doomed Dad's dastardly duo of drinks and drugs. Damn you, Death. Drown drunken with despair to be drained dry of your dreams. Down with the Devil I'll drag you one day to play with the demons and diseases. Duel me you dirty disgusting disastrous disappointment of a deity. Dusk or dawn, we'll display our dramatic dispute. Deny and discover how damaging deals can distinctively design your demise. Deliver yourself and deem my divine desire to despise and destroy. I delve decked with diamonds to derail the data that directs me to the dark den boundless with daunting delusionals and degrading deranged. Destiny defends my side as your dogma I'll divide with your defeat, so I may drive to a valid destination.

the Odd wheel

The third wheel on a tricycle carries forward.
Dragging the other two wheels behind it
waiting for them to split off so it could be free to
go onward on its own.

But one wheel alone proves to be unstable with
nonstop attempts to balance.

The spare tire on an automobile is a tool.
Hanging on the back
while the other four tires carry onward.
Its only use comes when one of those four tires
breaks down
and help the others continue.
But once the other tire is patched,
or they find a suitable replacement,
the spare is tossed right back.

The world only spins one way.
Wheels are made in pairs,
Tires are made in even groups,
Both drive forward or are carried forward.

So who will spare the odd wheel?

Fool Me Once

Fool me once, its shame on you
Fool me twice, its de ja vu
Fool me thrice, now that's not nice
Fool me four, I yell no more
Fool me five, am I alive
Fool me six, I need a fix
Fool me seven, already eleven
Fool me eight, it's far too late
Fool me nine, I'm far from fine
Fool me ten, it's time this ends

End it all
and look up to see the passing light
only to fall back to darkness
and start over
back to you
where you fool me once, and its de ja vu

The True Sin

Is it Pride?
Our stubbornness that forces us to never adapt?
To never know our limits and just accept them?

Is it Sloth?
Our laziness that we try to confuse with efficiency?
To follow a shortcut to the path of least resistance?

Is it Greed?
Wealth in material and knowledge that knows no bounds?
To willingly bring harm for personal gain?

Is it Lust?
The extreme lengths we will go to satisfy our desires?
To believe all our actions are justified in the name of what we seek?

Is it Gluttony?
A void that only expands the more we attempt to fill it?
To never understand when enough is enough?

Is it Envy?
Resentment for others who started behind and finish ahead?
To stand still and wallow in what could've been?

Is it Wrath?
Unresolved fury waiting for one misplaced fuse to blow up the world?
To lose all sense and reasoning where friend and foe become one?

It is Existence.
A constant state of awareness for an undeniable truth.
To live and accept that no matter how much we're akin, no one is without sin.

To The Top

0 feet up, can’t even see the end.
The rocky surface slopes outward away where the destination isn’t visible.
I wonder if I'll make it.

100 feet up, the rhythm is set.
My callused fingers grip and pull at the rugged mineral surface.
It isn't so bad.

200 feet up, realization hits me.
I’m no longer inside the gym protected by floor pads, walls, or even a rope.
Breathe and relax. Just don't fall.

300 feet up, now past the halfway point.
The first strain pulls my muscles while standing on a small gravel shelf.
Don’t slip. Don’t slip. Please, don't slip.

400 feet up, the finish is in sight.
My fingers are raw like sandpaper, and blood begins to trickle from my nails.
It's there. Just go. It's there. Just go. It's there. Just go!

500 feet up. I made it.
I turn to see the beautiful landscape that most only see through a screen.
There's nothing like the real thing.

Blaze, Blade, and Blood

Sparks ignite the night
As flames dance along the bridge
Cauterizing wounds

The sharpest steel forged
Slicing wind, severing bonds
My own extension

Scorching grounds run red
Crimson waves wash bloodied blades
And the world goes blind

Apocalyptic Limericks

Everything is just peachy
When white robes become preachy
Ignore the rest
Cause I'm the best
As 'Vini Vidi Vici'

Casualty counter is high
Chaos created is nigh
Streets running red
Littered with dead
Shattering your peace goodbye

And now come the withered grains
Blackened bread brings ashy veins
Masses shall starve
Tombstones I carve
Rumbling chorus entertains

Always wishing to extend
But skin turns pale in the end
Reap what you sow
Grasp what you know
And greet me like an old friend

At last Judgement arrives

Now where will these souls revive
Exceed with wings
Or fall with kings
Or question if they'll survive

Renaissance

At 6 years old, I stroll through the medieval faire
with my parents.
Accepting a glass worm made by dragons.
Aweing at all the colorful characters
And eating the fluffy cotton candy with fresh
cool water.
Coming across a small market stand with foam
weaponry of all types
For slicing and dicing and slashing and dashing.
I ask the strange man, "Can I have that sword
please?"

At 12 years old, I stroll through the medieval
faire with my friends.
Accepting a glass worm made by blacksmiths.
Donning a single red and black tabard
And chewing on a sizeable salty turkey leg with
cool enough soda.
Coming across a market stand with wooden
weaponry of all types
For slicing and dicing and slashing and dashing.
I say to the old man, "I would like to have that
short sword, good sir."

At 21 years old, I stroll through the medieval faire.
Accepting down the glass piece made by a glassblower.
Strutting along with full black leather, the swashbuckler hat, and steel-toe boots
And drinking bitter-sweet beer from my metal flask by the gulps.
Coming across a large market stand with iron and steel weaponry of all types
For slicing and dicing and slashing and dashing.
I parley with the elderly vendor, "I shall have that fine longsword, honored smith."

At 60 years old, I stroll through my kingdom.
Handing out glass worms to the little ones entering my grounds.
Strolling through as those bow down in respect of the crown on top of my gray head,
And sipping the finest wine from my golden chalice.
Coming across my merchants with foam, wood, and metal weaponry of all types
For slicing and dicing and slashing and dashing.
I proclaim to them all, "Treat thy weapons well.
The future depends on them."

sand

How much can it endure?
How does something once so whole persist after
being eroded to almost nothing?
How does something remain when both man and
nature strike it down time after time?
Once large and jagged now small and coarse.
Or heavy and smooth now weightless and rough.
Or vast and beautiful now vast and irritating.
So easy to crumble if not picked up right,
but hidden mysteries hide underneath the surface
waiting for someone with patience and passion
to dig them up.
But all they care about is the water.
The same pretty water that's constantly crashing
onto the unwashed masses.
Escaping the waves to still get stepped on by
those without thought.
It's desperate to be whole again
clinging on to those who step on them in hopes
to reach higher places
only to be wiped and washed away once again.
Its only strength is to cling to each other.
Connect with all pieces of itself to form any
structure it so desires.
But even together,

against the strongest pressures and hottest fires,
it only becomes more see-through.

Unlucky

Consider yourself unlucky waking up before your alarm,
but consider yourself lucky waking up at all.
Consider yourself unlucky forgetting your phone,
but consider yourself lucky not needing it.
Consider yourself unlucky stubbing your toe,
but consider yourself lucky to be walking.
Consider yourself unlucky hearing a crying child,
but consider yourself lucky they aren't crying at you.
Consider yourself unlucky paying rising gas prices,
but consider yourself lucky driving a car.
Consider yourself unlucky failing class,
but consider yourself lucky understand why.
Consider yourself unlucky no longer a best seller,
but consider yourself picking up the pen.
Consider yourself unlucky receiving the minimum prize,
but consider yourself lucky winning any prize.
Consider yourself unlucky losing the game,
but consider yourself lucky playing.

Consider yourself unlucky losing grandma,
but consider yourself lucky she passes
peacefully.
Consider yourself unlucky loving someone who
doesn't love you,
but consider yourself lucky loving is something
you can do.
Consider yourself unlucky suffering pain not
inflicted by you,
but consider yourself lucky it wasn't worse.
Consider yourself unlucky crashing rock bottom,
but consider yourself lucky willing to climb out.

Cold Call

It's been a while since we talked.
I sit quietly and await your call.
A couple months ago, you arrive at Alaska.
Thousands of miles from the sunshine.
You in cold, me in hot.
You with mountains, me with grasslands.
It was described as another world.
Stuck with family to move around like nomads,
It hasn't stopped our late night chats.
You always said you couldn't wait to be 18,
To finally move into one spot by yourself and anchor down.
But there was a point in time when we both were in the hot grasslands.
For years running through fields in the blazing heat.
For years people saw you with me and me with you.
For years we planned our futures, even our retirement.
I never thought those years would change so abruptly.
I wait for my phone to flash and fly to it like a moth.

I wait for your name to appear on the screen and
a smile to form on my face.
I wait
and wait
and wait...

Question

Ask a question.
My intelligence is no question.
The knowledge I possess, passed on from
professor after professor.
My mind is one.

Ask the question.
My wisdom is vast.
The experience I lived, laughed, and loved
throughout my journey to the center and back.
My body is one.

Ask the question, please.
My charisma is verse as you can see.
The verse of my arsenal of words, intimidation,
my sword, persuasion, my curse.
My soul is one.

Who.

Who?

Who do you think I am, as I am a man with no
need for no plan?

What.

What?

What do you think I do as I roam this very planet just like you?

Where.

Where do you think I go as every hill and mountain has a summit?
And when do you think I'll get to it living in the present in the presence of others?

Why.

Why?

Why...I don't know.

stuck

All the times I drove you home, sharing the lives
we lived.
Our shared interests in horror movies and
murder mysteries.
Our shared love for dogs and hatred for
humanity.
Our upbringings were vastly different, but
Our compatibility as two people is stronger than
steel.
And I wanted more.
I still do.
You say you did too, but
I was too slow.
Once again, I let fear stall my courage to tell you
what I wanted.
A problem fixed, but too little too late.
"Thank you for telling me" was always the
response.
But it isn't a proper answer,
leaving me in constant confusion.
That's why I compromised.
I want you in my life,
and you claim to need me in yours.
So I stuck myself the forever friend zone.

While you are with someone who could be the one that you end with.
You love him.
I understand that, but can't accept it.
I understand that he was there a couple of months before I officially came into your life
I understand that love works in mysterious ways, and you can’t help who you are attracted to.
I understand that these feelings I have will forever hold onto my heart, preventing true acceptance.
Forever stuck in a never-ending cycle of what could’ve been.
Forever to be contempt with minimal satisfaction.
Forever in Purgatory.

Experiment

Does the mouse know it's in a maze?
Does the frog live happily before dissection?
Does the guinea pig realize the world outside?

What about me?
What is my test subject number?
What test am I to be subjected to today?

Am I in the control group?
Am I the one injected?
Am I the injection?

Is this the goal?
Is there a goal?
Is this a defect?

Am I the outlier?
What is this elevated feeling?
You know what screw these rules.
I play my own game! Run my own experiments!
I hypothesize that I control what I do.
Now let's run some tests, shall we...

These results are incredible!

I conclude that I am the controller of my own
creation!

But wait...

What if this was the experiment all along?
What if I'm the virus in the dish of bacteria?
What if my self-awareness spreads and creates
mass hysteria?

Is it right to follow my heart?
Is it wrong to purposely disrupt the results?
Is it easier to conform to the test?

look into the fire

Wind carries the air we breathe.
Water brings the hydration we need.
Earth gives us a foothold in this world.
Yet when we play with fire we only get hurt.

The smoke smogs the air,
The ashes rain on the oceans,
The flames scar the ground,
Yet it also depends on the others.

It depends on Wind to deliver oxygen to breathe.
It depends on Water to douse it when getting too hot.
It depends on Earth to spread and roam the landscape.
Yet they don't depend on it to survive.

We can still suffocate,
We can still drown,
We can still choke,
Yet we don't wish to be burned.

The destruction it possesses,
The volatility of its nature,
The chaos it represents,

Yet it still's necessary for life.

It provides warmth,
It provides light,
It provides a chance to rise,
Yet we will always fear it.

I don't fear running into the burning building.
I don't fear setting my heart ablaze.
I don't fear being reborn in ashes.
Yet I lack the moments to do so.

Primal

Never forget the inner force within you.
A door that can only be unlocked with a certain key,
And the price is high.

It's that first time you taste blood.
Your body beaten and battle-worn to your limits.
Only then can you make the choice.

Your thoughts go silent as the flames of fury consume the mind.
Your veins expand as heat and adrenaline rush through.
Your inhibitors turn off to release your full power.

Awaken the instincts that protect you.
Remember the muscle memory driven into them for millennia
The will to survive at all costs.

Every hurdle can be jumped,
Every wall can be climbed,
Obstacles become minor annoyances.

Become a double edge blade.
Taking as much as you are giving.
Only the will to complete your goal drives you
forward.

Once the task is complete, the door will shut.
The toll will be paid in full,
But you will have finished what you started.

a moment that never comes

Fists bash the bag.
Skin splits open.
Bruises mark on the knuckles.
Yet I'll never fight.

Feet collide with concrete.
Legs rush forward.
Blisters peel off the pads.
Yet I'll never flee.

Fingers press on paper.
Ink drying fast.
Stories form on the pages.
Yet I'll never finish.

Brain searches for serenity.
Nerves calm down.
Thoughts flow through the neurons.
Yet I'll never find.

I'll overcome any obstacle.
Mind stays sharp.
Body ready for the moment.
Yet I'll never force.

Ballad of Kythos

Gather round, gather round,
Rest around the fire.
As I regale a tale
Of a demon's pyre.

A figure of shadow
And controller of flame.
With dual-wielding sabers,
They all know him by name.

It's Kythos Amakus,
The savior of sin.
Cursed at birth by demons,
It's where it all begins.

With their blood in his veins,
He gains all their power,
But with horns and a tail,
The commoners cower.

But Kythos isn't one
To back down from a fight.
For monsters kill monsters
Until the morning light.

After slaying a beast
One day out of the blue,
A courier arrives
Says, "A letter for you."

The parchment is royal,
Calligraphy in ink,
but it was signed in blood,
It made Kythos rethink.

His presence requested
By a local town's count
To work along his side,
Payment to be surmount.

Kythos trusted instinct
Over anyone's word.
As he can clearly see
The true offer is blurred.

Nonetheless he accepts
To uncover the truth,
And save the town's people
While sparing the youth.

So onwards he travels,
His swords close to his fists.
Only to discover
A town trapped in a mist.

As soon as he enters
He's overcome with dread.
It wasn't long after
He's attacked by the dead.

Kythos slashes and burns
Ending them all with ease.
But trying to exit,
He learns he cannot leave.

A set of bloody eyes
Appearing from behind.
A grim voice says to him,
"Looks like you've been confined."

Kythos faces the man
And instantly had known
Without seeing their grin
That The Devil had shown.

"So about my offer,"
The Devil asks smugly,
"If you come to refuse,
Then things could get ugly."

Kythos starts his assault
With shadow, blades, and flame.
But despite his attacks,

The Devil had remained.

"Disappointing I say,
I was expecting more."
With almost no effort,
Kythos was on the floor.

"You will remain alive,
You just have to submit
But until you accept
Your stay, is permanent."

The Devil fades away
Kythos lays in defeat.
But that did not stop him
from getting on his feet.

Kythos must discover,
And reach to new levels
For his tools of darkness,
Won't affect The Devil.

After searching for long
In The Devil's domain,
He comes across an elf,
Both alone and in pain.

Paranoid beyond help,
The elf attacks Kythos.

Though with his injuries,
The battle wasn't close.

But while at death's door,
The elf gains clarity.
He whispers his last words,
"You are the remedy."

With the last of his life,
He gave Kythos a blade.
The first time in his life,
Kythos had received aid.

The Devil had returned,
and Kythos was ready.
For once since coming here,
He stood his ground steady.

The Devil asks again
"So what's it gonna be?"
Kythos smiles and says,
"Your death, I guarantee."

He unsheathes his new blade,
Which radiates the night.
Forged by solar magic,
It emits the sun's light.

The Devil gives a wince

at the blade's sudden sight.
But grins with a blood rush,
"Now this will be a fight!"

Demon versus Devil
The battle shook the Earth.
At the end of their duel,
Kythos had proved his worth.

A devastating blow
Makes The Devil submit.
For Kythos's prowess
He was forced to admit.

He fled to his castle,
and never had returned.
The Devil was vanquished
No longer a concern.

The mist had been lifted
And the townsfolk were free.
For who their savior was,
A demon not foreseen.

But his celebrate was short
As tragedy struck then,
For Kythos Amakus
had met a delayed end.

Succumbing to his wounds
The demon passed away.
But the tale of Kythos
Is still regaled today.

www.ingramcontent.com/pod-product-compliance
Lightning Source LLC
LaVergne TN
LVHW052104160826
845678LV00015B/3362

* 9 7 8 9 3 5 7 4 4 0 7 4 5 *